476
Decorative Designs
CD-ROM and Book

John Leighton

DOVER PUBLICATIONS, INC.
Mineola, New York

The CD-ROM on the inside back cover contains all of the images shown in the book. There is no installation necessary. Just insert the CD into your computer and call the images into your favorite software (refer to the documentation with your software for further instructions). Each image has been scanned at 600 dpi and saved in six different formats—BMP, EPS, GIF, JPEG, PICT, and TIFF. The JPEG and GIF files—the most popular graphics file types used on the Web—are Internet-ready.

The "Images" folder on the CD contains a number of different folders. All of the TIFF images have been placed in one folder, as have all of the PICT, all of the EPS, etc. The images in each of these folders are identical except for file format. Every image has a unique file name in the following format: xxx.xxx. The first 3 or 4 characters of the file name, before the period, correspond to the number printed with the image in the book. The last 3 characters of the file name, after the period, refer to the file format. So, 001.TIF would be the first file in the TIFF folder.

Also included on the CD-ROM is Dover Design Manager, a simple graphics editing program for Windows that will allow you to view, print, crop, and rotate the images.

For technical support, contact:
Telephone: 1 (617) 249-0245
Fax: 1 (617) 249-0245
Email: dover@artimaging.com
Internet: **http://www.dovertechsupport.com**
The fastest way to receive technical support is via email or the Internet.

Bibliographical Note

476 Decorative Designs CD-ROM and Book, first published in 2005, is a new selection of designs from *1,100 Designs and Motifs from Historic Sources,* by John Leighton, first published by Dover Publications, Inc., in 1995. The plates are originally from *Suggestions in Design, Being a Comprehensive Series of Original Sketches in Various Styles of Ornament. Arranged for Application in the Decorative and Constructive Arts,* first published by D. Appleton and Company, New York, in 1881.

Dover Electronic Clip Art®

International Standard Book Number: 0-486-99685-9

Manufactured in the United States of America
Dover Publications, Inc., 31 East 2nd Street, Mineola, N.Y. 11501

001

002

003

004

005

006

007

008

009

010

011

012

013

014

015

016

017

018

019

020

021

022

023

024

025

026

027

028

029

030

031

032

033

034

035

036

037

038

039

040

041

042

043

044

045

046

047

048

049

050

051

052

053

054

055

056

057

058

059

060

061

062

063

064

065

066

067

068

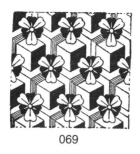

069

070

071

072

073

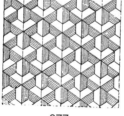

074

075

076

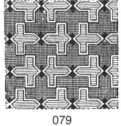

077

079

078

080

081

082

083

084

085

086

087

088

089

090

091

092

093

094

095

096

097

098

099

100

101

102

103

104

105

106

107

108

109

110

111

112

113

114

115

116

117

118

119

121

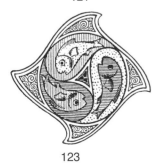

123

124

120

122

125

126

127

SANS PEUR EN AVANT FER · SANS REPROCHE ·

128

129

130

131

TRIS IN UNO · IUNCTA

132

FOR THOU SHALT... WATERS

LIGHT ON

133

134

135

136

137

138

139

140

141

142

TRIA
JUNCTA
IN UNO

143

144

145

DIEU ET MON DROIT

146

147

148

149

150

151

152

153

155

154

156

157

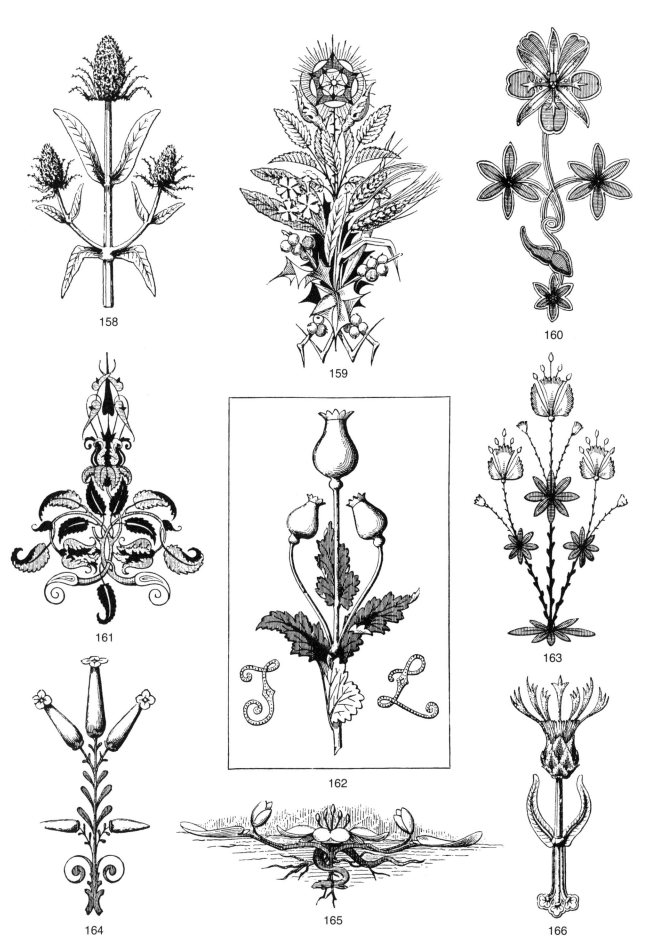

158

159

160

161

162

163

164

165

166

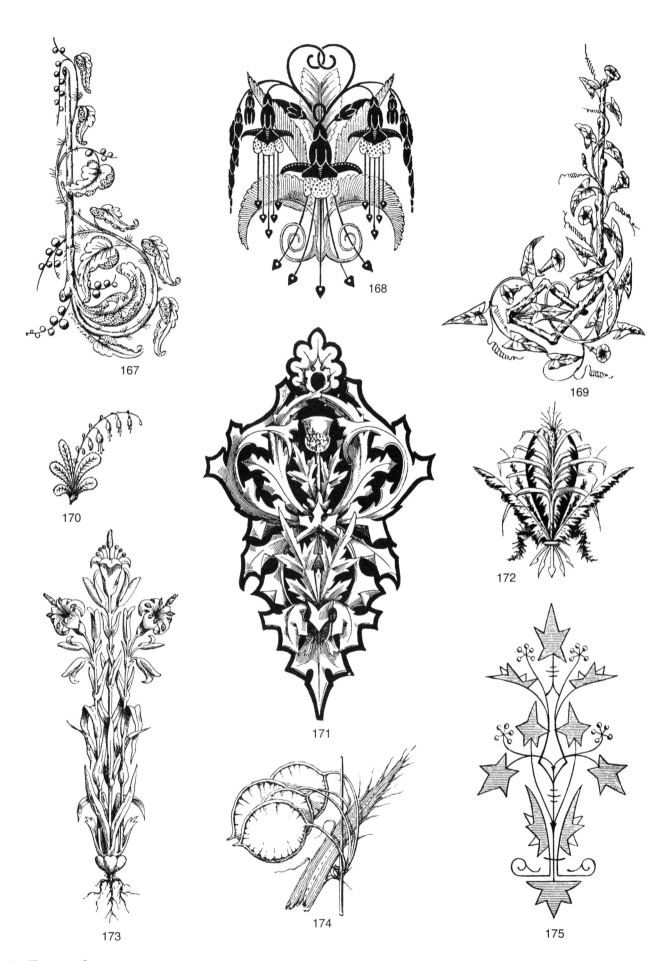

167

168

169

170

171

172

173

174

175

176

177

178

179

180

181

182

183

184

185

186

187

188

189

190

191

192

193

194

195

196

197

198

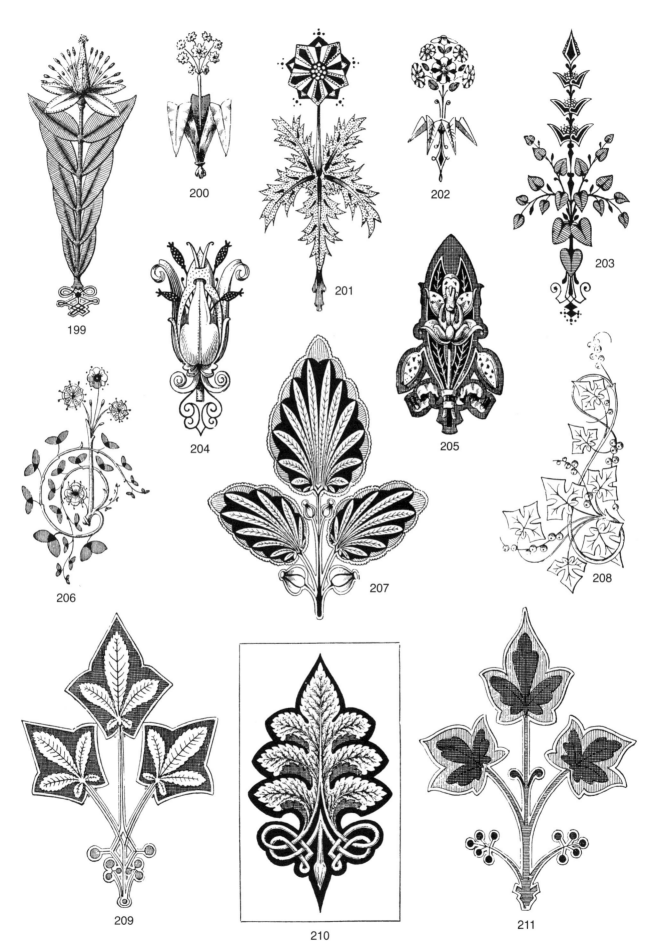

199

200

201

202

203

204

205

206

207

208

209

210

211

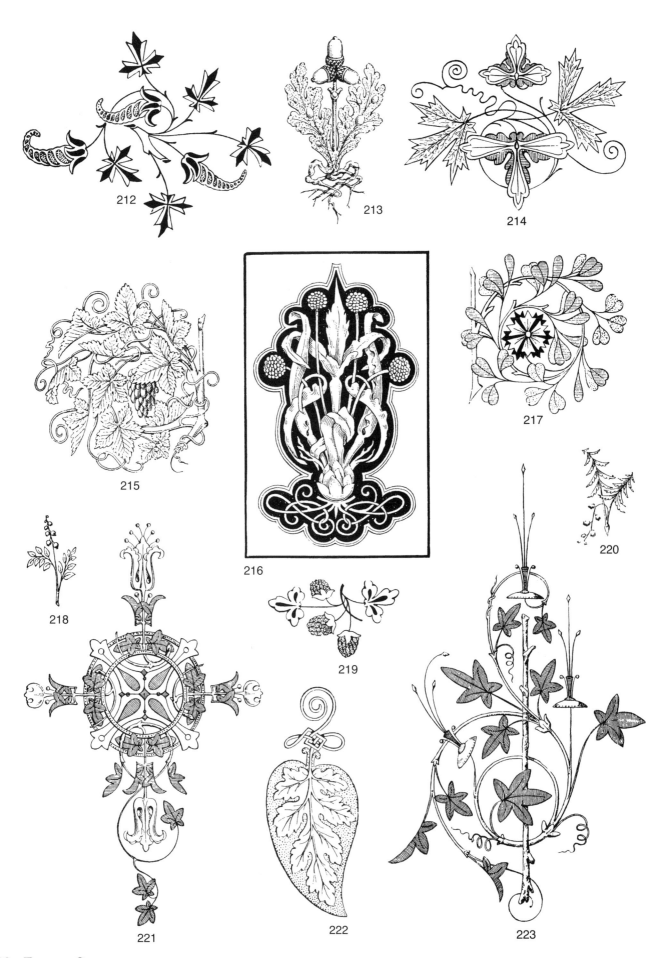

212

213

214

215

216

217

218

219

220

221

222

223

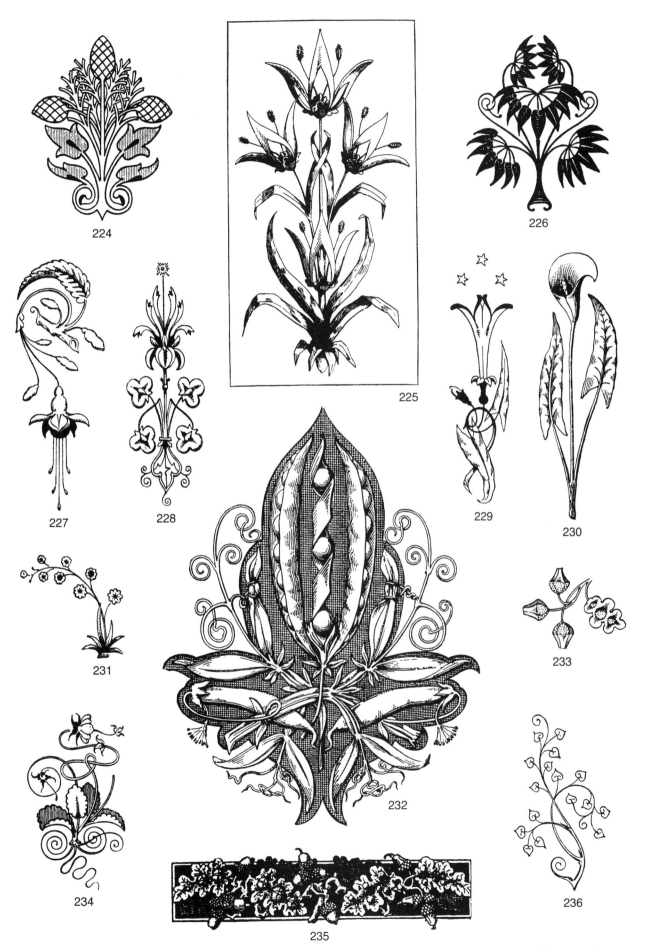

224

225

226

227

228

229

230

231

232

233

234

235

236

237

238

239

240

241

242

243

244

245

246

247

248

249

250

251

252

253

254

255

256

257

258

259

260

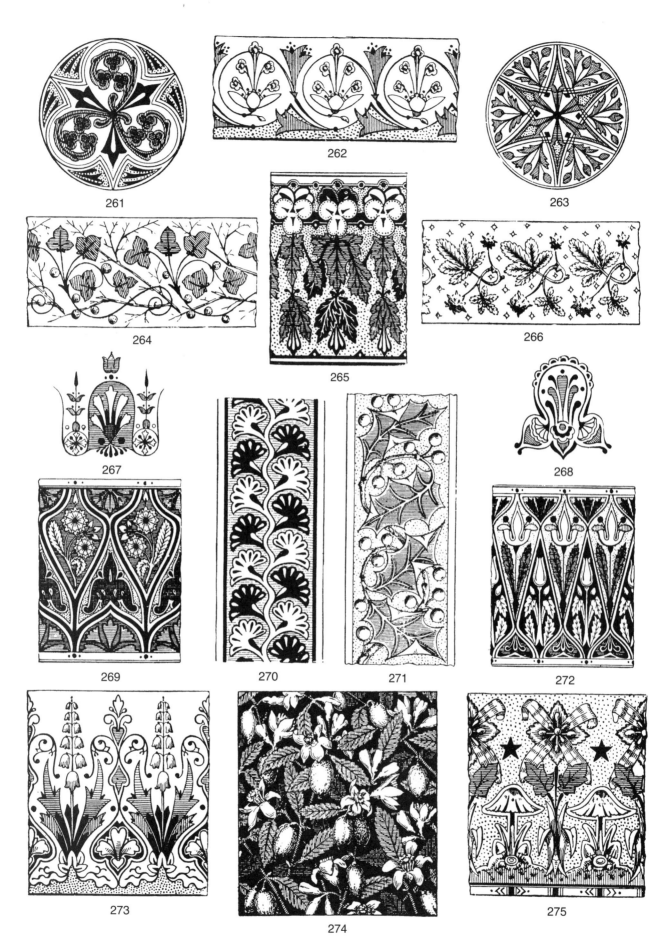

261

262

263

264

265

266

267

268

269

270

271

272

273

274

275

276

277

279

278

280

281

282

283

284

285

286

287

288

289

290

291

292

293

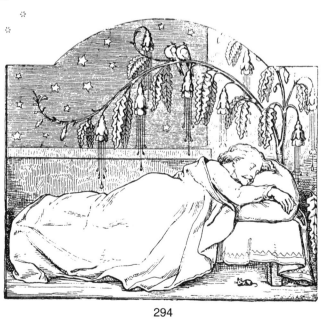

294

295

296

297

298

299

300

301

302

303

304

305

306

307

308

309

310

311

312

313

314

315

316

317

318

319

320

321

322

323

324

325

326

327

328

329

330

331

332

333

334

335

336

337

338

339

340

341

342

343

344

345

346

347

348

349

350

351

352

353

354

355

356

357

358

359

360

361

362

363

364

365

366

367

368

369

370

371

372

373

374

375

376

377

378

379

380

382

383

381

384

385

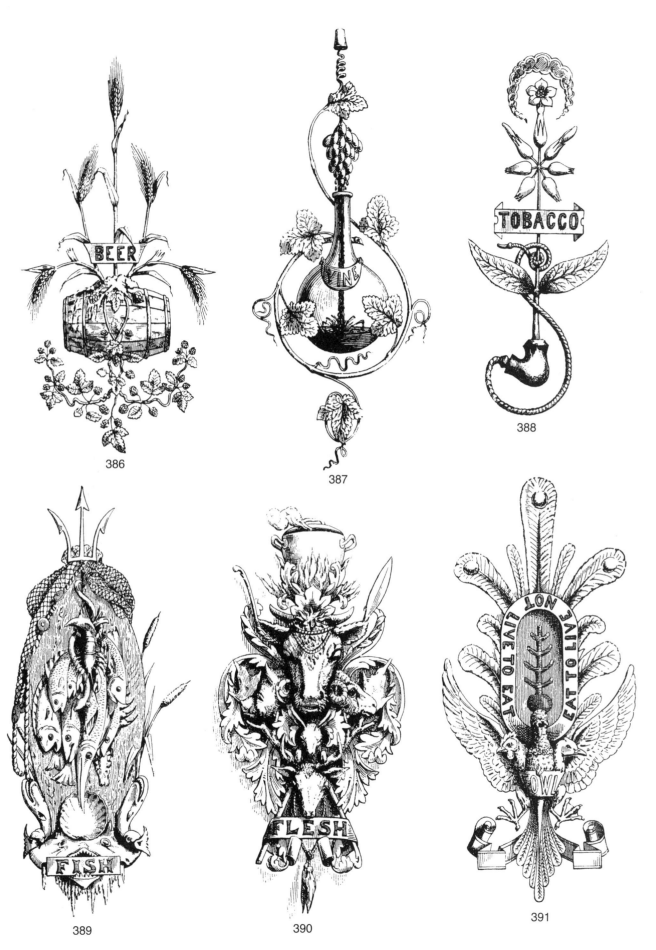

386

387

388

389

390

391

392

393

394

395

396

397

398

399

400

401

402

403

404

405

406

407

408

409

410

411

412

413

414

415

416

417

418

419

420

421

422

423

424

425

426

427

428

429

430

431

432

433

434

435

436

437

438

439

440

441

442

443

444

445

446

447

448

449

450

451

452

453

454

455

456

457

458

459

460

461

462

463

464

465

466 467 468

469 EGYPTIAN 470 ASSYRIAN 472 GRECIAN 473 EUROPEAN

471

474 475 476